D1708213

GRAPHIC LIBRARY™

GRAPHIC EXPEDITIONS

INVESTIGATING MACHU PICCHU

AN *Isabel Soto* ARCHAEOLOGY ADVENTURE

by Emily Sohn

illustrated by Cynthia Martin and Barbara Schulz

Consultant:
Dr. Thomas Brown
Professor of History
Augustana College
Rock Island, Illinois

Capstone
press®

Mankato, Minnesota

Graphic Library is published by Capstone Press,
151 Good Counsel Drive, P.O. Box 669, Mankato, Minnesota 56002.
www.capstonepub.com

062010
005833R

Books published by Capstone Press are manufactured with paper
containing at least 10 percent post-consumer waste.

Library of Congress Cataloging-in-Publication Data
Sohn, Emily.
    Investigating Machu Picchu : an Isabel Soto archaeology adventure / by Emily Sohn ;
illustrated by Cynthia Martin and Barbara Schulz.
    p. cm. — (Graphic library. Graphic expeditions)
    Summary: "In graphic novel format, follows the adventures of Isabel Soto as she explores
the history and culture behind the Inca city of Machu Picchu" — Provided by publisher.
    Includes bibliographical references and index.
    ISBN 978-1-4296-3407-6 (library binding)
    ISBN 978-1-4296-3894-4 (softcover)
    1. Machu Picchu Site (Peru) — Comic books, strips, etc. — Juvenile literature.
2. Graphic novels. I. Martin, Cynthia, 1961– ill. II. Schulz, Barbara (Barbara Jo), ill.
III. Title. IV. Series.
F3429.1.M3S64 2010
985'.37 — dc22   2009001173

Designer
Alison Thiele

Cover Artist
Tod G. Smith

Colorist
Michael Kelleher

Media Researcher
Wanda Winch

Editor
Christopher L. Harbo

Photo Credits: Shutterstock/Johnathan Esper, 8; Joel Shawn, 11; Jason Scott Duggan, 20

Design Elements: Shutterstock/Chen Ping Hung (framed edge design); mmmm (world
map design); Mushakesa (abstract lines design); Najin (old parchment design)

TABLE OF CONTENTS

Cliff dwellings, Arizona, present day

Hello? Anyone home?

Actually, the American Indians who lived here abandoned these cliffs long ago.

But they left things behind.

These artifacts show us how people lived in these cliffs.

People then weren't that different from us. They cooked, played games, and made art.

To an archaeologist, even the smallest trinket can open a window into the past.

Machu Picchu, present day

We're at an elevation of more than 7,800 feet, or 2,380 meters.

No wonder I'm dizzy. Coming to such high altitudes can cause altitude sickness.

Tell me more about this amazing place.

Check out this map.

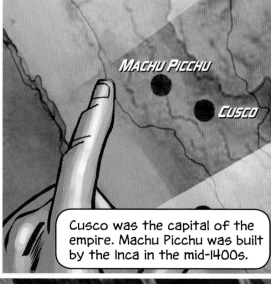

A people called the Inca originated in Peru between AD 1000 and 1200. They eventually controlled a nearly 3,000-mile, or 4,800-kilometer, span of the Andes Mountains.

MACHU PICCHU

CUSCO

Cusco was the capital of the empire. Machu Picchu was built by the Inca in the mid-1400s.

THE ANDES

The Andes are the second highest mountain range in the world. Some peaks are taller than 20,000 feet (6,100 meters). Conditions at those altitudes can be windy and cold. The terrain is rough, and earthquakes are common.

ASHLAR CONSTRUCTION

The Inca used a construction method called ashlar. In this technique, stone blocks fit together so tightly that there are no holes or spaces between them. The Inca's work was so precise that no mortar was needed to hold the stones in place.

Machu Picchu, 1911

According to my calculations, this should be Machu Picchu in 1911.

This must be what it looked like before Hiram Bingham arrived.

SNAP!

RUSTLE!

RUSTLE!

Someone's coming! I'd better hide!

13

Maybe this was a sacred place, Hiram. Perhaps the Inca gathered here for important religious ceremonies.

Stones like these were used in other Inca cities.

Maybe it was a farming village where they grew crops.

In many tropical climates, terraces are built to create flat fields on steep hillsides.

It could have been a military fort. They would have seen enemies coming from miles away up here.

Perhaps this city was the final refuge of the Inca. Maybe they retreated here during the Spanish conquest of Peru in the 1500s.

More about Solstices

Solstices happen when the earth's axis is tilted the most toward or away from the sun. On the summer solstice, the earth tilts toward the sun. It receives more hours of sunlight on the summer solstice than any other day of the year. On the winter solstice, the earth tilts away from the sun. It receives the fewest hours of sunlight on the winter solstice. In South America, the summer solstice is in December. The winter solstice is in June.

THE INCA TRAIL

The road leading from Cusco to Machu Picchu is called the Inca Trail. It is a popular route for tourists. The route starts about 50 miles (80 kilometers) from Cusco. It ends at Machu Picchu. Tens of thousands of tourists spend two to four days hiking the route every year.

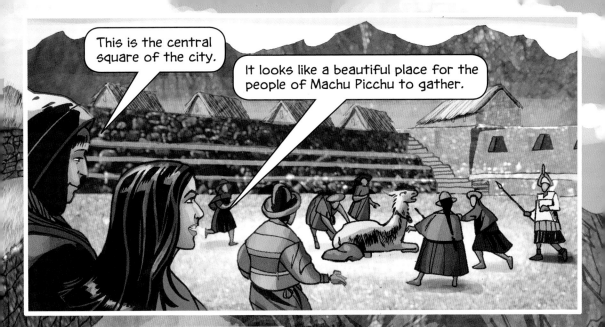

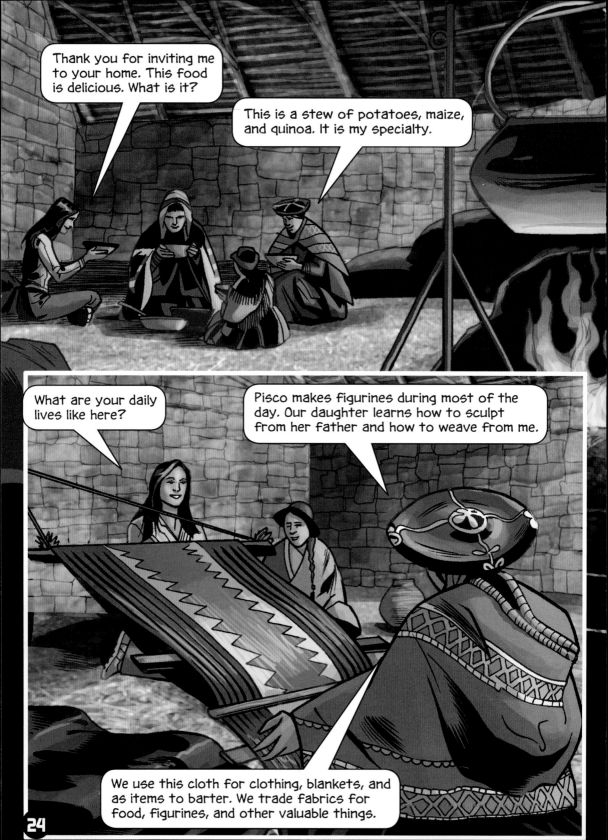

Machu Picchu, present day

It looks like I'm back in the present. Now, where's Dan?

Izzy, you're back!

Hi, Dan. I had quite an adventure!

What did you find out?

Figurines like your golden llama were important. But they were fairly common.

I met an artisan named Pisco. He gave this figurine to me as a gift. It matches yours perfectly.

MORE ABOUT MACHU PICCHU

In the Inca language, "machu" means old or ancient, and "picchu," means peak or mountain. Together, Machu Picchu means "ancient mountain."

In Inca societies, adult men paid their taxes with work. They worked for the government a certain number of days each year. Their skills determined whether they built bridges, served in the army, made pottery, or did other tasks for the state.

The Inca culture flourished for more than 300 years. But in 1531, the Spanish invaded Peru to search for gold. With horses, armor, steel swords, and guns, they defeated the Inca. In 1533, the Inca capital of Cusco was taken by the Spaniards. Spanish forces captured the last Inca ruler in 1572.

Machu Picchu is often called the "Lost City of the Inca." It earned this name because the city was hidden by jungle vegetation until Hiram Bingham arrived in 1911.

Bingham brought thousands of artifacts from Machu Picchu to Yale University. These artifacts included mummies, bones, and other valuable objects. For many years, the Peruvian government said the objects belonged to Peru. In 2008, Peru announced a plan to sue Yale University to get many of the artifacts back.

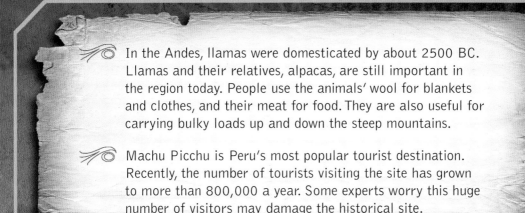

In the Andes, llamas were domesticated by about 2500 BC. Llamas and their relatives, alpacas, are still important in the region today. People use the animals' wool for blankets and clothes, and their meat for food. They are also useful for carrying bulky loads up and down the steep mountains.

Machu Picchu is Peru's most popular tourist destination. Recently, the number of tourists visiting the site has grown to more than 800,000 a year. Some experts worry this huge number of visitors may damage the historical site.

MORE ABOUT

NAME: Dr. Isabel "Izzy" Soto
DEGREES: History and Anthropology
BUILD: Athletic   **HAIR:** Dark Brown
EYES: Brown   **HEIGHT:** 5' 7"

W.I.S.P.: The Worldwide Inter-dimensional Space/Time Portal developed by Max Axiom at Axiom Laboratory.

BACKSTORY: Dr. Isabel "Izzy" Soto caught the history bug as a little girl. Every night, her grandfather told her about his adventures exploring ancient ruins in South America. He believed lost cultures teach people a great deal about history.

Izzy's love of cultures followed her to college. She studied history and anthropology. On a research trip to Thailand, she discovered an ancient stone with mysterious energy. Izzy took the stone to Super Scientist Max Axiom, who determined that the stone's energy cuts across space and time. Harnessing the power of the stone, he built a device called the W.I.S.P. It opens windows to any place and any time. Izzy now travels through time to see history unfold before her eyes. Although she must not change history, she can observe and investigate historical events.

GLOSSARY

altitude (AL-ti-tood) — how high a place is above sea level

archaeologist (ar-kee-OL-uh-jist) — a scientist who studies how people lived in the past

artifact (ART-uh-fakt) — an object made and used by people in the past

artisan (AR-tuh-zuhn) — a skilled worker, especially one whose occupation requires hand skill

barter (BAR-tur) — to trade food or goods and services instead of using money

civilization (siv-i-luh-ZAY-shuhn) — an organized society

domesticate (duh-MESS-tuh-kate) — to tame an animal so it can live with or be used by humans

empire (EM-pire) — a large territory ruled by a powerful leader

irrigate (IHR-uh-gate) — to supply water for crops using channels or pipes

maize (MAYZ) — a type of corn

mortar (MOR-tur) — a mixture of lime, sand, water, and cement that is used for building

refuge (REF-yooj) — a place that provides protection

sacred (SAY-krid) — holy or having to do with religion

solstice (SOL-stiss) — the days of the year when the sun rises at its northernmost and southernmost points

terrace (TER-iss) — a raised, flat platform of land with sloping sides

READ MORE

Croy, Anita. *Solving the Mysteries of Machu Picchu.* Digging into History. New York: Marshall Cavendish Benchmark, 2009.

Ganeri, Anita. *The Incas.* Ancient Civilizations. Minneapolis: Compass Point Books, 2007.

Kops, Deborah. *Machu Picchu.* Unearthing Ancient Worlds. Minneapolis: Twenty-First Century Books, 2009.

Richardson, Gillian. *Machu Picchu.* Structural Wonders. New York: Weigl Publishers, 2009.

Shuter, Jane. *The Incas.* History Opens Windows. Chicago: Heinemann Library, 2009.

INTERNET SITES

FactHound offers a safe, fun way to find Internet sites related to this book. All sites on FactHound have been researched by our staff.

Here's all you do:

Visit *www.facthound.com*

FactHound will fetch the best sites for you!

INDEX